LONDON
AND ITS
BUSES

LONDON TRANSPORT

55 Broadway, London, S.W.1.

LONDON has been growing ever since it first sprang up on the banks of the River Thames in Roman times. By the Middle Ages the old walled City of London was the trading centre of England and much of the world. Two miles up-river from London Bridge was Westminster, home of Kings, Court and Parliament. By the year 1800 both these original settlements had swollen, spilling across the Thames into Surrey and forming one built-up town in which dwelt around one million souls.

In those days there was little need for local public transport. The rich, who liked to live in the fashionable West End – where now stand the shops and offices of Mayfair, St. James's and Westminster – either owned carriages or hired them, just as today we hire taxi-cabs. The poor – who generally dwelt in overcrowded and insanitary conditions near their work – had neither need nor money for such a luxury. For though London was the largest and most important town in the Kingdom, it was still small enough to get around comfortably on foot.

After 1800 London continued to grow – but faster now, for more and more people were moving in from all over Southern England. And as London grew, so also did the ranks of a new social class, a moderately well-off lower-middle class. These clerks, tradesmen and skilled mechanics could afford something better than a cramped room in a 'rookery', yet the West End was beyond their means. In growing numbers they moved to the outskirts and the villages surrounding London, where the air was cleaner and new terraced homes were being built. Every morning these early commuters walked into the City from Paddington, Islington and Walworth, just as their descendants come in today from further afield.

Although walking remained for many years the most common way of getting to work, those who could afford it took to using a carriage or local stage-coach to shorten their journey. This was very expensive, however, and not always convenient, for within the older parts of London public stage-coaches were restricted by law.

By 1829 there were one and-a-half million people living in London, and there was now a distinct need for something cheaper and more flexible than stage coaches; a vehicle that would pick up and set down passengers other than at a few fixed points, and without their having to book seats in advance. So it was then, having seen horse-buses in Paris, that George Shillibeer began running his elegant, single-deck 'Omnibus' on 4 July 1829.

At first, Shillibeer's bus ran every three hours, from Paddington Green and along the present Marylebone, Euston and Pentonville Roads to the 'Angel' Islington, then down City Road to the Bank. It was inevitably an immediate success; Paddington was at that time farther from the Bank than any other part of built-up London, and the area was being developed for just the sort of person who could afford Shillibeer's shilling fare. At that time few Londoners earned more than one pound a week.

Shillibeer's bus seated twenty passengers, facing each other inside a box-on-wheels pulled by three horses. By the standards of the day it was large – later horse-buses were smaller and usually pulled by two horses – but the general design was not unknown. What was interesting about the 'Omnibus' was that it stopped on demand for casual passengers and that its fares were significantly lower than cabs or local stage-coaches, although in real terms Shillibeer's bus was more expensive to ride in than today's taxi.

Within two years there were ninety buses following Shillibeer's original route and other services had also started. From 1832 – when the law was changed to allow buses to operate throughout London – more and more routes were opened up. Londoners learned very quickly to hop on a bus.

Poor George Shillibeer, however, had been declared bankrupt by this time. After a few more years transporting the living he turned his attention to the dead and finally found success as a funeral director.

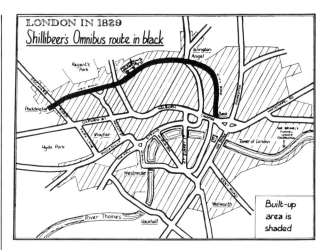

1829 George Shillibeer's first elegant bus was drawn by three horses between Paddington Green and the Bank. Its crew was dressed in Paris fashions! These frills did not last long, and the buses which soon joined it were simpler vehicles, pulled by two horses. Shillibeer's shilling fare was equivalent to today's five pence, although seventy-five pence was considered a good weekly wage in 1829.

1850 From about this time the first double-deck horse-buses appeared in London, but it was quite a climb up to those sideways-facing seats on top. Proper stairs and forward-facing seats came in the 1880s.

1890 The best-known form of the London horse-bus, pulled by two horses and carrying twenty-six passengers. Bus-horses worked for about three hours a day, with a short rest every half-mile, but crews could be on the road for up to fifteen hours daily.

1910 After several years of experimental (and temperamental) petrol-buses, the famous B-type entered service, carrying thirty-four passengers. The various types of London bus are given letter codes, which you can see on the bonnet or side of the bus. The B-type was mass-produced in the 'General's' own workshops at Walthamstow with easily interchangeable parts – important in the repair shop. Its reliability enabled new bus routes to be opened up all round London, and many were used by the military in France during the 1914–1918 war.

1919 Once the First World War was over, bus development really began moving. This 'K' carried forty-six passengers, all facing forward for the first time. The 28 horse-power engine is the same as that fitted to the B-type, but now the driver sits beside it.

1925 Covered-top buses came to town, although police regulations had delayed their use in London. This bus – the NS – had a specially lowered chassis, for easy boarding and alighting, but the driver still had no windscreen.

London continued to grow throughout the nineteenth century and the number of horse-buses in service increased steadily. Slowly their design improved. Right from the start passengers were allowed up on the roof beside the driver at a reduced fare – just as they had on stage coaches – and from around 1850 proper seats began to be fitted, back-to-back facing outwards down the centre of the roof. A more conventional double-deck arrangement, with forward-facing roof seats and a proper staircase and rear platform, followed in the 1880s.

Throughout the nineteenth century buses were painted all sorts of colours and permanently marked with distinctive names showing which route they followed. Many services were run by groups of bus operators – called 'Associations' – who controlled the number of buses on each route, preventing too much competition.

From 1855 a new company began buying up horse-buses in London, for bus operation was profitable in those days. The London General Omnibus Company – or 'General' as it was usually called – soon owned most of the eight hundred buses then running in London. From that time onwards it was always the largest bus company in London.

Though railways came to London in the 1830s, it was not until 1863 that the first underground line was built through London, roughly following the route of Shillibeer's first bus. Throughout the nineteenth century, however, trains seem to have catered for a different sort of passenger. Sherlock Holmes, for example, was a frequent rail traveller but never took a bus, choosing a hansom cab or brougham instead. Even later, the famous Raffles only went by bus when in some appropriate disguise, although Father Brown well knew his way around London by bus.

More significant competition came after 1870 from the new trams but, happily for bus-owners, trams were never allowed to enter Central London. Instead they concentrated their services in the suburbs and quickly established themselves as working-class vehicles. Until the turn of the century, buses concentrated on the middle classes who could afford their higher fares, never offering the special cheap tickets that trams and trains provided for 'workmen'.

By the 1890s – when the population of Victorian London had grown to four million and its built-up area stretched out to Streatham and Blackheath, Hammersmith and Tottenham – the horse-bus had evolved to its final form. The box-on-wheels now carried twenty-six passengers – twelve inside and fourteen on top – at an average speed of five miles-an-hour, and by 1901 there were more than three-and-a-half thousand of them on the streets of London between eight in the morning and eleven at night. But their days were numbered; long overdue, the first mechanically driven buses were already carrying Londoners into the Edwardian era.

There had been serious experiments with buses powered by batteries, steam or petrol engines since the 1890s. By 1904 the first reliable petrol-buses were in regular service, and a year later it was plain that the future lay with them. Nevertheless, steam-buses ran in London until 1919 and petrol-electrics until 1934. A variety of buses entered service in those first exciting years of the twentieth century; Straker-Squires, Milnes-Daimlers, De Dion Boutons, Wolseleys and Clarkson Steamers among them. Along their sides were painted boldly the names of their operators; Vanguard, Great Eastern, Union Jack, Tilling and General were among the better known.

With the new mechanically-powered buses came a new outburst of competition between London buses. Once again the 'General' took steps to regulate the industry, and after a series of amalgamations and agreements the London General Omnibus Company was by 1913 in a stronger position than ever.

Early petrol-buses carried thirty-four passengers in what was essentially a lengthened horse-bus body mounted on a rigid chassis – an underframe to which were attached solid-tyred wheels and engine. The driver sat behind his engine, unprotected from the weather, holding a steering wheel instead of reins.

Of all these early petrol-buses one stands out above the rest. Introduced in 1910, more than three thousand of the famous B-type bus were built. Although looking little different from its predecessors, the B-type set new standards of reliability, and it came on to the road at just the time when the 'General' needed to expand.

For a new stage in London's development was beginning. Still expanding, the built-up area now reached out to independent market towns such as Bromley and Croydon. Since the 1890s municipal housing had been built in the suburbs with the deliberate intention of lowering the population of overcrowded Central London. Not only the middle-classes 'commuted' now, so also did the working-classes in ever increasing numbers, although they were turning to the municipal tram and train, two competitors with whom the 'General' had no agreements.

The B-type enabled the 'General' – hub-to-hub with its associated operators – to extend its network outwards, often alongside rail and tram services, and it was doing so quite effectively when the First World War was declared. Many B-types went to France, and for the next few years expansion was halted.

From 1919 until 1929 new and bigger bus designs appeared regularly in London. Successive changes placed the engine beside the driver, allowed forward-facing inside seats, lowered the chassis frame and placed a roof over the top deck. Along the way, pneumatic tyres came into use. Improvements generally followed the relaxation of controls by the Metropolitan Police, who were rather conservative about bus design at the time, with the result that certain modern features did not appear in London until long after they were common elsewhere.

For a short time after the end of the First World War there was a shortage of buses in London, and from 1922 new operators came on the road. Once again the 'General' eliminated competition as far as possible by buying it out, but many of these independently owned buses continued running until 1934, adding colour to the streets and meanwhile teaching the 'General' and its associates some useful lessons.

The between-wars period was interesting in many ways, not least because it saw London's buses and their route network finally come of age. All around London considerable house-building was taking place, often on a vast scale. 'By-Pass Tudor' and 'County Hall Cottage' housing appeared, lining and surrounding new arterial roads, and there was a growth of light industry in the suburbs. More and more bus routes were opened up in suburban and outlying areas, and the previously close-knit London bus map began changing into what it is still: over-lapping networks of local routes superimposed on a frame of longer trunk routes. Some of these longer-distance routes now started in the country around London, becoming 'Green Line' express coach services.

Adapting to change, suburban buses tended, more and more deliberately, to 'feed' passengers into the improving local rail services, and fixed stopping places – bus stops – spread all over London. Yet another sign of those changing and competitive times came with the general operation of buses much earlier in the morning than had been the case before 1914, together with certain all-night services. As its original clients began turning to the motor car, so the bus began seriously to attend to the needs of London's working-classes, who also benefitted from the lower fares that larger buses made possible. The formula was successful, and year after year London's buses carried more and more passengers.

During the 1920s a theory was developed that the growing operations of London's variously-owned transport services would improve if they were better co-ordinated. In 1933 a form of amalgamation was finally achieved. Within a radius of roughly twenty-five miles of Trafalgar Square – enclosing a population of more than nine million people – control of six thousand buses, two thousand trams and many local railway lines was passed to a new and independent public authority, known ever since as 'London

1925 Pneumatic tyres were allowed only on single-deckers at first, but from 1928 the police also sanctioned them for double-deckers. This single-deck 'S' dates from 1923; most 'S' types were double-deckers.

1929 Yet another step forward came with the introduction of the larger, six-wheeled 'LT' in 1929; some were still running twenty years later. The radiator on this bus was the first of more than 10,000 similar and distinctive AEC radiators that can still be seen on a few London buses in 1979.

1930 Although the London General Omnibus Company – the 'General' – operated the majority of London buses, there were many privately owned buses running in London from 1922 to 1934. At first these independent buses ran only on routes where it was easy to make money, and some did so with little real concern for their passengers. Later on, however, the independent operators opened up some useful new routes and brought buses to London that were equal to – and sometimes better than – the General's. This Leyland was made in the workshops of the largest private operator, the City Motor Omnibus Company.

1934 Only fifteen years after the 'K' appeared, the first really modern bus went into mass-production for London. The 'STL' – first built in 1932 – was now given a diesel engine and a freshly designed and attractively finished body carrying fifty-six passengers. The two small stencil plates immediately beneath the first lower saloon window told inspectors from which garage the bus came and its numbered place in the timetable for each route. Although slightly modified now, this is one of many peculiar features of today's London bus that can be traced back for many, many years.

1943 During the Second World War buses were in short supply and built to very austere standards. Passengers had to sit on wooden slatted seats, and sometimes there was no back window upstairs. These measures reduced the need for skilled labour and scarce materials. The white mudguards on this Guy were intended to make it stand out in the blackout; all London buses were marked thus from 1939 to 1945.

1947 Almost seven thousand famous Regent Three – 'RT' – buses were built for London between 1939 and 1954. They are probably the best known of all London's buses. These 'RTs' show one of the idiosyncracies of London buses in the past; on some batches their route numbers would sprout from the roof. London's buses have always carried more route information than is normal elsewhere, originally at the request of the police.

Transport'. In the outer ring of its domain, the new organization sympathetically coloured its buses a rural green, but throughout the built-up area of London the now-familiar red paint – used by the 'General' since 1907 – soon appeared on buses everywhere.

London Transport was able to concentrate on improving not only services, but also vehicles, and by 1934 the earlier 'General' designs had evolved into a recognizably modern double-deck London bus which promptly went into mass production. Based on a standard AEC chassis, but powered by a diesel engine, it carried fifty-six passengers – considered for many years afterwards the most that one London conductor could handle. The attractive and well-finished steel-framed body of this bus – designed and built in London Transport's Chiswick Works – used efficiently for the first time all the space within the box-on-wheels.

Single-deck buses have always been in a minority in London, and until 1929 they had generally been simple adaptations of double-deckers, but to them the 'General' and now London Transport gave attention. The result was three unconventional designs which operated successfully in some numbers in London, but they were mechanically too advanced for their time. Equally advanced, but more traditional in design, was a new double-decker that came from Chiswick Works in 1939. Known as the Regent Three – or 'RT' – only a few were built, for Britain at war had more immediate uses for its aluminium and skilled coach-builders. Though no-one realised it at the time, the golden days of London's buses were already over.

At the end of the war London's buses were old and tired. Wartime maintenance had been kept to a minimum and few new buses had been delivered. Suddenly, however, everyone wanted to travel by bus, for there were not many cars about and petrol remained rationed. London Transport tried hard to recover the years it had lost but, despite boosting services with several hundred hired coaches and buses, for some time there simply weren't as many buses on the road as there should have been.

Experience with mass-producing 'Halifax' bombers during the war encouraged Chiswick Works to redesign the 'RT', although London Transport was no longer allowed to build buses after it was nationalized in 1948. The new RT was jig-built and a vast improvement on the first models, with components made to such close tolerances that most parts would fit any of the seven thousand RTs that were made between 1947 and 1954. This simplified the keeping of spare parts and reduced the need for expensive skilled labour in garages.

The new buses first replaced worn-out vehicles and allowed services to be improved, then, from 1950 they began triumphantly replacing the remaining London trams. Even while they did so the bubble suddenly burst. After more than a century of steady market-growth, the impossible had happened. In 1952 London's buses carried fewer passengers than in 1951. If the red double-decker has a heart, that was surely when it came nearest to breaking.

The downward trend has continued ever since. Travel is for most people a means to an end, and public transport a less than perfect second best. High wages and full employment in the 1950s and 1960s encouraged many people to buy cars and brought about changes in Londoners' leisure habits. Twice-weekly trips to the cinema turned into evenings in front of the television, and weekend outings were now taken in the family car. Quite simply, as time went on, more and more people found they could do without the bus.

Improved wages have also allowed more Londoners to buy their own homes, but high prices and improved rail services have often encouraged them to move up to one hundred miles away from the capital in which they continue working. Others have left for New Towns, and all the while the population of inner London was falling.

The result was a dilemma which still continues. For several years after its passengers began dwindling, London Transport continued running services as if they might one day return, but in the struggle to cover costs, service reductions finally began in the late 1950s and have continued at intervals ever since. Growing traffic congestion, continued staff shortage and, more recently, mechanical difficulties have also affected the quality of service operated and still do so.

During the 1960s London's buses began to visibly adapt to the changing times. The last 'RT' had been built in 1954, and in that same year the first of London's next generation of buses began a lengthy test programme. Entering full service from 1959, the new 'Routemaster' was also jig-built, but without a chassis – instead the body was given extra strengthening. The Routemaster was the last of a long line of buses built specially for London, and the most adaptable – a unique blend of standardization with flexibility. Early specimens carried sixty-four passengers, but later models were 'stretched' to carry seventy-two. The Routemaster kit was also adapted to produce front-entrance buses and, finally, one with its engine at the back. The last link with the horse-bus was broken.

The rear-engined Routemaster was a belated acknowledgement by London Transport that, technically excellent though the standard version undoubtedly was, the bus with an open rear platform was already outdated by the standards of many major bus operators. Changes in government policy prevented further development of the rear-engined Routemaster; it remains regretably unique.

Since 1965 London has bought standard rear-engined buses, with doors at their front entrances and carrying up to eighty-nine passengers. They have not always proved as reliable as earlier designs, either in London or elsewhere. 'Off-the-shelf' single-deckers have also come to London since 1965. With these new buses – on which the driver often sells tickets – has come a new pattern of routes concentrating services even more on distinct local neighbourhoods.

As planners re-shaped post-war London and highway engineers tried to unclog traffic jams, it became obvious that neither were paying sufficient attention to the needs of the bus. Services and stopping places were moved away from where they suited passengers, and the efficient use that buses made of scarce road-space was often overlooked. From 1964, however, special bus lanes and other measures have helped to combat congestion. A better deal for London's red buses followed from 1970 when the Greater London Council, the elected authority responsible for planning and roads, was given control of their finances and general policy. London Transport was also given a subsidy to help its operations – common enough abroad but rare at that time in Britain. In the 1970s, too, came free bus travel at certain times for London's elderly.

The 'social' function of buses was clearly acknowledged, but the question that must one day be resolved was already being asked; what is the proper level of bus services needed in London and who should pay for it?

However effectively London's buses adapt themselves to change – and the continued and growing emphasis on the local role of buses demonstrates London Transport's continuing commitment to the community – bus travel will continue to decline, unless living standards fall or our traffic-choked towns become too much for us to accept. Nevertheless, there will always be those who choose to use buses or cannot drive; particularly for children, the elderly, the poor and the handicapped, the bus will always be needed.

One of the ironies of recent years is that, while there are fewer buses in service, their routes cover more roads than ever before. In the suburbs most people have a bus service nearer their homes than they did ten years ago – though conversely, as the population has moved out of inner-suburban London, many services are now withdrawn from those areas at slack times. Some parts of London which previously never saw a bus are now served by the very latest sort of service. The buses are small, single-deckers, with twenty-six seats. They operate less frequently than normal services and will stop almost anywhere to pick you up or set you down. The Londoner of 1829 would recognise the principle.

After 150 years the 'Omnibus' is still very much alive!

1959 The Routemaster was the last bus designed especially for London and the last with its entrance at the back. It is one of the most reliable buses ever used in London, though strangely, it was the first double-decker to be built with heaters for passengers. The Routemaster was also the first bus to be fitted with an automatic gear box and air suspension.

1965 Buses with their engine at the back – instead of at the front where the horse had been – became popular in Britain from 1960. Government policy and the trend to operating buses on which the driver collects fares have obliged London Transport to buy such buses since 1965, although they suffer the disadvantage that you cannot get on and off them between stops – important in London, where short-distance riders have always been encouraged.

1968 The single-deck bus has become more common in London since 1968 than ever it was before, and many have been used to operate special short routes in Central London or 'neighbourhood' routes in the suburbs.

1979 This is the Metrobus – one of the very latest rear-engined double-deckers coming onto London's streets. The passing Routemaster shows just how much the appearance of London buses has changed over the last twenty years.

First bus out

Half-past-three in the morning. A double-deck bus stands near the narrow arched entrance to a North London bus garage. It rocks gently as the conductor steps on to the platform.

The driver's door slides shut, and lights inside the bus dim briefly while its 11.3-litre diesel engine turns over, then fires. With a hiss of air from its gearbox, the empty bus draws slowly away, past lines of darkened houses towards nearby Stamford Hill Circle.

White exhaust hangs in the still air beside it while the bus pauses for its first great-coated passengers, then moves off again. The 3.33 a.m. Route 243 to Holborn is on its way—the first London bus of the day.

Ready for the run-out, Victoria Garage, 1978 △

△ Bus preparation and signing-on

Into service, Cricklewood Garage, 1911 ▽

Between five and seven o'clock more and more buses leave London Transport's 67 garages, carrying early morning passengers to work, and all night workers home.

This is the time when garage staff work hard to ensure that every bus has a crew, and every crew has a bus fit for the road.

All being well, by eight o'clock the full rush hour service of over 5000 buses is on the road.

Until around 1900 there were very few buses in service before eight o'clock, and the rush hour barely existed.

△ West Croydon, 1964

△ Trafalgar Square, 1931

London Wall, 1978 ▽

8

△ The Old Lady of Threadneedle Street, 1934

Kingsway Underpass, 1970 △

Fleet Street, around 1890 ▽

△ Full up outside, 1907

▽ King's Cross, 1938

Bow Church, 1933 ▽

10

▽ Luxury coaches help out when new buses are scarce, 1948

Congestion in Trafalgar Square, 1924 △

▽ London Bridge Station, 1961

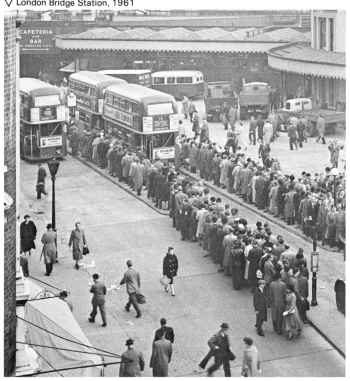

△ Streatham, 1978

Borrowed buses, Morden, 1949 ▽

11

Among rush hour passengers in the past were some whose job it was to build buses. Until 1967, most London buses were made in the London area, at first in local coach-builders' yards, and later in special works—at Walthamstow (from 1910) and at Southall (after 1927).

Until 1933 the AEC bus building company was owned by London bus operators. They were able to order just the type of bus they wanted, and this useful relationship continued into the 1960s.

In the 1920s and 1930s London Transport's own Chiswick Works built more than 5000 bus bodies.

In recent years London buses have been built in the West Midlands but some are now being assembled in West London.

◁ New chassis, 1923   Body-building at Chiswick Works, 1938 △

▽ New Green Line coaches ready for service, 1938   Completed Routemaster leaves the body-builder, 1959 △

From about nine o'clock the pressure slackens, although in recent years the issue of free passes to old folk and the increasing number of visitors to London have put new and welcome demands on London's bus services once the rush hour ends.

Less welcome has been the growth in general traffic levels, for congestion is now common in many parts of London at almost any time of the day.

Until the 1950s, when the five-day working week became common, there were rush hour services on Saturdays—in the morning and at lunch-time.

∇ Strand, 1923   Solid tyres in bad repair, Duncannon Street, 1933 △

▽ Summer in the City, 1922   △ St. Clement Danes, 1886   St. Paul's Cathedral, 1970 ▽

Garage only

As the rush hour ends, many buses return to their garages, for during most of the day only two-thirds of London's bus fleet is needed to provide adequate services.

By nine o'clock many bus crews have done half their day's work. For some this is a chance to relax before returning to duty again for the evening rush hour.

Battery-bus returns to its depot, 1907 ▽

▽ Grooming the bus-horses

▽ Garage shunter in wartime, 1940

Canteen, around 1910 ▽

Keeping the wheels turning

Most of the essential maintenance needed to keep London's buses on the road is done in garages during the day.

Until the 1920s, complete overhaul of buses was often done at garages, but today it is done elsewhere. In recent years, however, the job of maintaining buses has become more difficult, as new and more sophisticated vehicles have appeared.

Underneath the Arches; City Motor Omnibus Co. garage at Peckham, 1933 △

▽ Shepherd's Bush Garage, 1978

▽ Early mechanical washer, 1921

△ Docking bays, Victoria, 1949

Automatic bus-washing, Sutton, 1978 ▽

Well known London

London's first bus services ran through the City and West End, along streets that mostly have changed little.

Although large areas of land have been redeveloped and some new roads have been built, London's best known bus routes still run along the same streets, passing monuments and buildings that George Shillibeer would have little difficulty in recognising.

▽ Mansion House, around 1910   Whitehall, 1978 △

▽ Nelson's Column in the early 1920s

△ Piccadilly Circus, 1936

Oxford Circus, 1973 ▽

18

△ Whitehall, 1938   ▽ Buses temporarily diverted past Buckingham Palace, 1955   Law Courts, 1966 △

△ Kensington High Street, 1930

King William Street in the late 1880s ▽

20

Special services

As well as ordinary bus routes, London Transport also provides services to meet special or occasional needs.

Even in horse-bus days you could hire a bus for your private party, and London Transport has a long tradition of running special tours to places of interest.

Similarly, London busmen have for many years organized special bus outings for children who, in the past, might otherwise never have had a day at the sea.

Buses frequently replace train services while railway maintenance work is undertaken.

△ Char-a-banc at Windsor, 1925 Children's outing, 1927 ▽

Sightseeing tour; Piccadilly Circus, 1979 ▽

Coach with special luggage boot; Victoria, 1937 ▽

▽ Bus replacing train; Brixton, 1964

The crew

Twenty thousand drivers and conductors are needed to run London's red buses. Since 1950 London Transport has found it hard to recruit enough staff to keep all its buses running, and at times this causes services to run less frequently than anyone wishes.

In an attempt to improve bus services, since 1964 London Transport has been operating more and more red buses without conductors. Today almost half of London's rush hour buses have no conductor on board.

Women started work on the buses in 1915, when the first 'clippies', as the women conductors were called, were given jobs with Thomas Tilling. Not until 1974 did women first drive London buses in service.

Driver waiting for his bus, 1978 ▽

△ Horse-bus driver, 1910

△ Woman Conductor, 1940

Changing crews; Golders Green, 1926 ▽

Bus crews are trained at London Transport's Chiswick Training School, although much of their training is given 'on the road'.

It takes two weeks to train a conductor, and around three weeks to train a driver, according to how long it takes a person to reach the high standard needed.

A well known feature of London Transport's training school has always been the Skid Pan, where drivers learn how to control a skidding bus. In the early days of motor buses, when solid tyres and cobbled streets were the rule, skidding was very common, but fortunately today it is rare.

Conductors learning their trade, 1935 △

△ Trainee driver, 1977

△ On the Skid Pan, 1977

Chiswick, 1939 ▽

Central London today is the visitor's London, where people work, shop or are entertained. But the London that matters most to Londoners is the London they live in.

In Victorian times London was much smaller, and most people lived within walking distance of their work. For more than a hundred years, London has been growing outward, creating new suburbs and absorbing nearby towns and villages.

These are the suburbs where Londoners live: Alf Garnett's West Ham, Tony Hancock's Cheam and Lord Gnome's Neasden. In the suburbs the bus remains an essential part of life, especially for families without a car. It takes father to the station, children to school and mother shopping; grandma to visit and grandpa to the pub.

Although the number of suburban trips has fallen dramatically over the last few years, it is in the suburbs that London Transport has developed new services, bringing the bus nearer to more front doors than ever before.

△ Upper Clapton Road, 1978

Brixton, 1935 ▽

New LCC housing at Becontree, 1929 ▽

△ Unknown alley, mid 1920s   ▽ Shoreditch High Street, 1896   Aldgate, 1937 △

▽ Blackwall, 1973

Sloane Square, 1924 △

△ Elephant & Castle, 1936

Kingsbury, 1937 ▽

△ Swains Lane, Hampstead, 1978   ▽ Greenwich and the Cutty Sark, 1962   Shepherd's Bush Green, 1978 △

∇ Mill Hill, 1961   Stoke Newington Common, 1978 △

∇ Richmond Park, 1936   Golders Green, 1927 △

△ St. Paul's Road, Stepney, 1935

Belgravia, 1935 ▽

All change!

In the early days buses often started and finished their journeys at public houses, just as stage coaches had done. At that time pubs were open all day, and they were convenient places to wait. Often they had yards where buses could stand off the road.

This custom lasted well into motor-bus days, and even now you can still see the names of pubs on the front of London buses.

Today many London bus routes terminate at railway stations or special bus stations, so that passengers can change easily from bus to bus or bus to train. For bus crews, too, this is helpful, for that much-needed cup of tea is rarely far away.

Even so, with more than 300 bus routes in London, many buses finish their journey in little-known side streets, for finding somewhere to turn a bus round is not easy in London today.

Albion Tavern, Cambridge Heath, in the 1880s △

Red Deer, South Croydon, around 1910 △

▽ Kensal Rise Station, 1936

△ Oxford Circus – then called Regent Circus – around 1890

Finsbury Park Station terminus, 1923 △

△ Richmond Bus Station, 1939

Turnpike Lane Bus Station, 1968 ▽

On the road

However hard a driver works to keep his bus to time, he can never see what is happening elsewhere on his route. Traffic congestion alone is causing London Transport to cancel or cut short up to 3,000 bus journeys on an average weekday.

To keep services running efficiently and reduce the effects of delay, London Transport has 5,000 supervisors —many of them Inspectors—in garages and on the road all over London. Radios link buses and inspectors to special control points.

△ Inspector using radio, 1978

△ Is it time to go? 1910

Mile End Road, 1922 ▽

Almost every week in London, traffic is delayed and diverted because of processions and demonstrations. This is no new problem for London's buses, which are routed at those times along other roads to reduce delay to passengers.

State occasions and ceremonial, such as the Opening of Parliament and processions of visiting Heads-of-State, are well-known and traditional features of London life.

Remembering the Battle of Trafalgar, 1897 △

Trafalgar Square: ▽ Demonstrating against unemployment, 1932

33

Fog

Pea-soupers, they used to be called, and London was notorious for them until the 1950s. Dense, acrid fog was caused by the widespread use of coal fires and cooking-stoves, but nowadays few people in London have open fires.

In those days, when fog settled in, bus conductors frequently had to walk for miles in front of their buses, guiding the driver.

Because of London's flatness in the vicinity of the river, there have been occasions when the Thames has burst its banks and caused flooding. Plans are in hand to avoid this happening in the future.

△ Fog, Whitechapel Road, 1952

▽ Flooding, Great West Road, 1949

Rain, 1914 ▽

Steam bus, Trafalgar Square, 1915 △

..and Snow

Snow, also, causes less disruption to buses than it once did. Mechanical gritting of bus routes, and more vehicles on today's roads, help prevent snow settling. Modern tyres are also more efficient than solid tyres.

Desperate measures! △

▽ East Finchley, 1962

Strike

Twenty thousand car-workers downing tools for a day have no immediate effect on the rest of us. The same number of busmen striking for a day makes banner headlines; four million people have no buses to ride on and streets all over London are congested.

In fact, strikes are rare in the bus industry. They are usually brief and confined to one or more local areas of London, generally arising out of criticism of particular duties busmen have to work.

There have been notable exceptions. In 1891 the majority of London busmen struck for a week against the introduction of accountable tickets, and in May 1926 most London buses were off the road during the nine-day General Strike.

For four weeks in 1937 London was again without buses, and while they were locked in their garages a King was crowned.

The best-remembered London bus strike was for higher wages; it lasted for seven weeks in 1958 and achieved nothing, apart from convincing many Londoners to buy a car a little earlier than they might otherwise have done.

Strikers at Catford Garage, October 1936 △

Troops called in, May 1944 △

▽ Few buses ran during the General Strike; Oxford Street, May 1926

War: 1914

Wars have always had an effect on London's buses. In the nineteenth century bus-horses were commandeered for use by the military, and in 1914 this custom was brought up to date.

Soon after the First World War was declared, the Government began requisitioning motor buses to serve with the troops in France. In many cases drivers went voluntarily with their buses, for this was the first 'motorised' war and their special skills were rare at that time.

Eventually 1300 London buses crossed the English Channel, whilst another 300 were used for military service in Britain.

Joining up △

△ London buses at Boulogne

Wounded from the Dardanelles; Plymouth, 1915 ▽

Armistice, 1918 ▽

37

War:1939

This was the People's War, for everyone was involved—at home and at the front.

During the Second World War, London buses were not generally sent abroad, but they were used many times for evacuations and troop movements.

Throughout the war there was a black-out, which made night driving slow and difficult. Between August 1940 and May 1941, London was bombed almost nightly. Buses and their garages were damaged, and services were frequently altered to avoid bomb-damaged roads and buildings.

London's buses bore the scars of bomb-blast from 1940 onwards, most frequently shattered windows replaced by boarding. In 1944 and 1945, London once more suffered, this time from flying bombs and rocket bombs.

Throughout the war bus services were restricted to save petrol. Because production was concentrated on the war effort, few new buses were built and maintenance was postponed. Quite early in the war, London was forced to borrow buses from other parts of the country to keep its services running. Later on, as the bombing moved from London to other towns and cities, London buses were lent to help elsewhere.

Croydon Garage, May 1941 △

▽ War workers and war damaged bus; Sidcup, 1943

Bus borrowed from Yorkshire; London Bridge, October 1940 △

BETWEEN 4.30 & 7.30 P.M.
WAR WORKERS NEED THIS BUS
HAVE A HEART

38

Service restrictions, 1939 △

△ Balham, October 1940

Converted Green Line coach for US forces. ▽

△ The promise   Victory, May 1945 ▽

AMERICAN RED CROSS CLUBMOBILE "SOMEWHERE" IN GREAT BRITAIN.

"SIGHTED SINKERS—SANK SAME."

PASSED BY U.S. ARMY CENSOR No. 21 E.T.O. U.S.A.

9

Breakdown

Inevitably things go wrong sometimes in a bus fleet that travels 179 million miles in one year.

Mechanical breakdowns were common in the early days of motor buses, but there came on the road in 1910 the first of a long line of buses specially designed for London.

Reliability improved, and in those days it was still possible for a driver to carry out roadside repairs, for buses were petrol-engined and simple by today's standard.

Leaning a seat cushion up against the back of a disabled bus is a habit peculiar to London busmen, thought to date back to horse-bus days, when it was used to stop people boarding.

Accidents to London's buses are rare, but when they do happen, radio-controlled breakdown vehicles are standing by, capable of solving any problem. And on the rare occasions when buses do go under low bridges, it happens usually when they are not in service, without passengers aboard!

Roadside repairs, early 1920s △

△ On the road to Epping, 1915   During the General Strike; Southwark, 1926 ▽

△ Kennington, 1978   Scalped, 1962 ▽

Overhaul

Every week, around 40 buses go to London Transport's Aldenham Works—on the northern fringe of the capital—for overhaul or major repair work.

Fifty years ago buses had to be thoroughly overhauled and repainted every year, but gradually the period between overhauls was extended, as buses were more sturdily built.

Nowadays a bus is repainted and given any necessary attention when it is three or four years old. Towards the end of its sixth year on the road, the bus will be taken into Aldenham for a thorough overhaul and re-paint, giving it a second 'life' of four years or more. When it comes out, the bus will be as good as—sometimes better than—new.

Until recently, the London bus was designed to allow its body to be lifted clear of the chassis and engine for overhaul. When refurbished, the body could be replaced on any appropriate chassis.

Newer, rear-engined buses are not made to the same standards and cannot be separated.

▽ Lifting a body off the chassis, around 1946

Ensuring that they pass the 'tilt-test': 1913; 1929; 1949; 1971 ▽

▽ Making destination blinds, around 1930

Spraying a chassis, around 1960 ▽

▽ New and overhauled buses awaiting licensing; Chiswick, 1939

London's country

Although usually associated with built up areas, London buses have gone out into the country since the early days of motor buses. The country was much nearer then.

In 1905 buses ran briefly between London and Brighton, and from 1912—when red double-deckers first came to Windsor—services began operating to country destinations all around London.

Special weekend services were particularly popular right up until the 1950s, for private cars were still quite scarce.

From 1933 London Transport also operated green (Country Area) buses in outlying areas up to 30 miles from Charing Cross, and express Green Line Coaches linked one side of rural London with another. In 1970, however, these services were taken over by the National Bus Company.

Even today, London's red buses can still be found as far afield as St. Albans and Caterham, Brentwood and Leatherhead.

Queueing for Box Hill; Clapham Common, around 1920 △

Crossing Putney Heath, 1928 △

▽ On the edge of Epping Forest, 1926

▽ Paying the driver, 1934

Eccleston Bridge, Victoria, 1937 △

▽ Bus for narrow country lanes, 1964

Sevenoaks, 1962 △

▽ Special bus for low bridges; Westerham, 1962

Bank Holiday

In days gone by the working week was six days long and summer holidays were often unknown.

But on four days in the Spring and Summer, factories, shops and offices shut down and Londoners took a day off.

In their thousands they flocked to Hampstead or Epping Forest or anywhere the sun shone and the air was clean, just to enjoy themselves for the day.

And the busman? He took his day off later, for a fine Bank Holiday (or Summer Sunday) could bring more buses on to the road than a normal day.

△ Chingford, Whit Monday 1939

Hampstead Heath, 1928 ▽

△ Windsor Castle, 1950

Off to the Derby, 1934 ▽

Street theatre is nothing new to London. In Victorian times the heart of the British Empire was alive with the sight and sound of street traders and entertainers. Organ-grinders, knife-grinders, boot-blacks and match-sellers; they knew that there was no gold paving in London.

After the first World War it was the turn of heroes fresh from France, and later still of unemployed miners who sang and played and sometimes even danced to bus queues before walking home—or back to cheap lodging houses.

Even today, behind the buskers and inscrutable players of strange musical instruments, there's a certain sadness. Why do they do it?

And just as London has always been a centre for street entertainers, so also it is for pageantry and the unexpected.

Music while you wait; Trafalgar Square around 1922 △

▽ Putney Bridge, around 1933

△ En route to the Tower, 1920

Sandwich-board men; Regent Street, 1909 ▽

▽ Parliament Square, around 1925

46

△ Preparations for a coronation; Westminster Abbey, 1911

Passengers

During 1977 London's red buses carried almost fourteen thousand million passengers. Put another way, this is as if everyone living in London went for two hundred bus rides during the year.

Of course, simple statistics are misleading. Some people never go on a bus whilst others use them every day. Buses in Central London are busy all day long, and people in inner-suburban areas generally ride on buses more often than those living further out.

Passengers vary, too, according to where they are and when they happen to be there. Leaving Victoria at nine o'clock on a Monday morning, a bus will carry office workers and shop assistants, glum and silent for the most part. An hour later, at Stratford Broadway, the atmosphere inside that bus will be quite different, mainly women going shopping, with a good number of old folk and a steady hum of conversation all contributing to the contented feel in the air.

And on Saturday night the jokers and the happy faces appear for a few hours; but where do they go for the rest of the week?

In 1951, when London Transport carried more people than ever before or since, thirty five thousand million passengers travelled by red bus, tram or trolleybus.* Since then, however, the population of London has steadily fallen and more and more people have bought cars, especially for pleasure trips. This is inevitable as society becomes richer.

But however many cars there are, there can never be roadspace for them all at the busiest times, and Londoners made it plain in 1973 that they do not want to live in a county criss-crossed by urban motorways. And there will always be the old, the young and the infirm who cannot drive, as well as those who choose to not have a car; for them, the bus will always be needed.

*Buses replaced trams from 1952, trolleybuses from 1962.

THE RIVAL OMNIBUSES.

The hazards of a crinoline, around 1850 ▽

Waiting, 1931 ▽

▽ The perfect passenger; Strand, 1937

◁ The descent, 1929

How not to do it, around 1920 △

▽ Coronation Bandsmen, 1953

△ Two minutes silence, Armistice Day, late 1920s

In the 1890s ▽

49

Over and under the River Thames

In 1815 London was small by today's standards (although far and away the largest town in Britain) but the built up area was mainly on the north side of the Thames. One of the reasons for this was that there were only three bridges over the river, at Westminster, Blackfriars and London Bridge.

During the years that followed, new bridges were built—including some for pedestrians only—and old ones replaced, but it was not until 1880 that all could be crossed without paying a toll.

The last bridge to be built on a new site—and the last you still see going down the Thames—was Tower Bridge, well-known for its twin towers, opened in 1894. In December 1952 a double-deck bus was crossing the bridge when its spans began lifting. Happily, the quick-witted driver was able to speed his bus over the gap before any serious damage was done.

△ Southwark Bridge, 1971

▽ London Bridge, around 1913

Waterloo Bridge. 1923 ▽

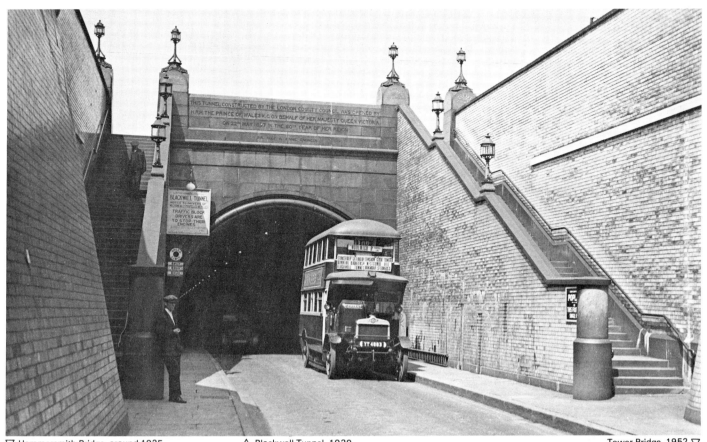

▽ Hammersmith Bridge, around 1925   △ Blackwall Tunnel, 1929   Tower Bridge, 1952 ▽

▽ Woolwich Free Ferry, 1951

O f all the stages in the evolution of the traditional London bus, one design stands out as a classic.

Called the Regent Three, and coded RT, it was a Chiswick thoroughbred right down to its hub caps.

Between 1939 and 1954 almost 7,000 RTs were built and fitted with elegant, carefully proportioned bodies. Although some were made a little wider than others, and for a while the designers weren't quite sure where the route numbers fitted best, all were unmistakably part of the same family.

Built of standardized and interchangeable parts, the RTs simplicity and reliability made it the most long-lived of all London buses. Many operated continuously for more than twenty-five years. Requiring a two-man crew, yet carrying only fifty-six passengers, they were economic anachronisms by the 1970s, turning whole areas of London into working transport museums.

But the RT carried on while buses half its age were retiring exhausted and broken, and London Transport was grateful for them. Now only a handful remain; already they are part of London's history.

△ Brand new; Clapham, 1940

Westminster Abbey, 1950 ▽

Replacing tramcars; Wandsworth Depot, 1950 ▽

△ Piccadilly, 1949   △ St. Paul's Cathedral, 1952   Oxford Street, late 1950s ▽

Evening rush

From three o'clock onwards the late-turn bus crews start signing on, and buses which have all day been straddling pits or standing idle begin to leave their garages.

The homeward flow begins early in the suburbs. Schools turn out and factories and works change shifts from around four o'clock, and by half-past-four the Central Area rush is on. Ninety minutes later it is all but over.

△ Stamford Hill Garage, 1978

▽ Aldgate, 1936

Regent Street, mid 1920s △

△ Full up! 1944

▽ Elephant & Castle, 1967

Park Lane, 1966 △

△ Bus lane, Piccadilly, 1973   △ Whitehall, 1926   Portland Place, 1978 ▽

London by night

At night London is transformed. The City falls into a dignified coma—for very few people live in the commercial heart of London—but the West End comes alive, a centre of entertainment and brash spectacle.

In the suburbs, far fewer pleasure trips are made by bus than was the case twenty-five years ago. Most people have television now, many local cinemas have closed, and there are new places to go, not easily reached by bus.

△ Parliament Street, Westminster, 1924

Regent Street, mid 1930s ▽

57

△ Fleet Street, 1978

Haymarket, 1964 △

Streatham Hill, 1978 ▽

Bromley Market Place, 1962 △

▽ Wapping, 1966

△ Regent Street, Christmas, 1965

Vauxhall, 1978 ▽

Who goes home?

London's buses run later than in most British towns and cities, for many services in the centre and suburbs operate normally until well after eleven o'clock.

Even after midnight, last buses are still leaving Central London on their final trip to a suburban garage.

Victoria Bus Station, 1978 △

▽ Boarding the last bus, around 1860

Victoria Embankment, 1965 ▽

◁ Big Ben, 1978

After the evening rush-hour many buses return to their garages. They are washed, and cleaned out and refuelled ready for the next day. Then, towards mid evening, the garage goes quiet.

Shortly after ten o'clock, a few at first, then progressively more of, the remaining buses arrive home. Conductors go to pay in and the mechanical washers begin turning again.

Around one o'clock the last one arrives and is put away, although sometimes it may have one more journey to make, taking home the staff that brought the last buses in.

Dorking Garage, 1938 △

Victoria Garage, 1947

Stockwell Garage, 1953 ▽

61

Night bus

As the last buses of the day return to their garages, the all-night buses come out. Their network of special routes, centred on Fleet Street and running far out into the suburbs, dates back to 1899, when all-night trams first ran in North London.

Right from the start the Nighters were intended for late and early workers, and many routes still don't operate on Saturday night.

Generally worked regularly by the same crews, the Nighters provide London Transport's most personal service, for buses have been re-timed and routes have been altered to suit the convenience of just one customer.

In fact, round the clock, every day and every night of the year—Christmas night excepted—there are red buses continuously on London's streets.

Night buses in Fleet Street, home of London's newspapers: 1923 △   1978 ▽

London buses are designed to last around fifteen years, but many have operated in the Capital for much longer.

Even when withdrawn from active service, useful work is often found for them.

In the past some were modified, becoming special-purpose vehicles; there have been circus-buses, cinema buses, and buses converted to towing vehicles and canteens.

Other have continued in use as buses, carrying passengers in various parts of this country and abroad, as far away as Sri-Lanka and Australia.

In recent years preserving old buses has become increasingly popular, and deservedly so, for they are an important part of our social and industrial history.

London Transport has its own collection of historic vehicles, going right back to horse bus days. From 1980 it will be on display in the centre of London, at Covent Garden.

△ Bus converted to tree-lopper, 1925

New use for an old double-decker ▽

△ Second-hand London bus in Doncaster, 1966

Two London buses in a rally line up; Sheffield, 1978 ▽

Scrap

In the past they were burned, for buses had a lot of wood in them. Nowadays the engines and gearboxes are salvaged—and often sent to the Far East for marine use—and the rest is melted down, for steel and aluminium go on for ever.

Around 2,000 London buses have been scrapped in recent years, at a place called Wombwell—the final irony, for the womb is the nearby furnaces of South Yorkshire's steel industry.

So look closely at that tin of beans or can of beer; perhaps it was on the 62s a few months ago.

△ Entering the scrap yard, Wombwell, 1978

Breaking up a horse-bus, Holloway, 1911 ◁

△ Waiting; Rainham, 1951

△ Going, going . . . 1978

. . . GONE, 1931